THE
REMAINS
OF
BURNING

LAUREN LOTT

Cover design by Islam Farid.
Special Thanks – Michael Lott and Glen Urane

I sat across from an Italian emissary,
this is what he told me.
'Write. Let your tears become
the waters that refresh others.'

This is how it goes.

First, the snatch of flame – the shaking, the breaking, the burnout, the death of a dream, the loss of a loved one, the line between before and after.

What follows is the cooling of coals –waking that can only be done in the absence of a flame; it's impossible to sleep when you're freezing.

In time, it is understood that ashes are of great value, and with courage, grief folds into gratefulness.

In writing, it is my intention to bring forth that which heals. And so, I offer these words, words for when what you thought would never happen, happens; words for when you feel all you have is the remains of burning.

CONTENTS

THE SNATCH OF FLAME.

First, hold your breath.
For disbelief swells high,
and to survive, you must deep dive,
and hope when you rise,
you will remember how to breathe.
For breathing is all you will be able
to do for a while.

-upon hearing the news.

I know, it is pain only felt,
never spoken.
So I will give you silence,
and sit beside you;
Spirit with Spirit.

We, each in our beds,
nursing our hearts,
trying to breathe.
We must remember,
our pain is not unique.
It belongs to all on the night watch.
And so, I think of you,
feeling as I do,
and I hope you think of me,
though you have never seen my face.

Pain is a crier;
a personal bellman.
He comes to awaken truth;
to show what is shakable,
and what is sure.
What comes and goes as a flame,
and what remains.

We deliver lost dreams one limb at a time;
wiping up the evidence of decomposing
desires month after month.
Though the stench of what used to live
in the womb of our heart lingers not forever,
there are little graves everywhere.

For all the burning,
there is a burning down.
For all the building,
there lays a crumbled town.
And now there's nothing,
no fire,
no lively flame,
but it is well,
now love can save the day.

It is the agony of one thousand arrows.
The emptiness of one million lonely nights.
A part of me is dying:
the part we called us.

Storms come.
Some water, some wash away.
All are in season.

Lonely heart unforgotten,
take peace and wrap it blanket-tight,
or use it to cover your ears,
so you cannot hear those tall stories that tower,
and tell you you've been left behind.
You have not been cast aside, but repositioned,
picked out for something rare and meaningful.

Maybe this pain is mercy.
Saving us from the shallows,
keeping us for tomorrows,
intentionally piercing our skin,
carefully knitting on wings.

Though you feel like dirt.
Disposable.
Disgraced.
Stripped of dignity.
Underserving of love.
You are worth,
the stars,
the moon,
the sea,
the earth.

-don't let the pain fool you.

Isn't it strange
how we try to hide
what costs the most.

-tears.

Revenge is a temptress,
pledging to heal; promising to put things right.
She is a trickster.
Her only want – to tie us in knots.
Hurting them will never heal you.

When I could go no further,
burn no more,
these two I discovered:
the end is the beginning,
and beloved ash is all I am.

This loss is birth,
and just like the body
of a new mother,
you will ache awhile.

Reject them.

-what to do with feelings of rejection.

What happened there
gave us new eyes,
and a heart for ones
we did not see before.

-pop goes the bubble.

Now and then,
life shifts to show us our strength,
and who is strong for us.

-only those who are free came running.

Cry,
but don't ask why.
No answer will satisfy.
Only know that when you feel
like you have been pushed into the earth,
you are growing up in the world.

Tears are the prelude.

Revolution starts within,
and pain is usually the instigator.

-the beginning feels like the end.

Sometimes we are pushed into corners
so we will learn to break down walls.

-a pathway no one knew was there.

Who quenched this flame?
I blamed a wicked wind,
before I looked up and saw
a thousand angels leaning down,
breathing out.

All that is shifting is sand.
All that is falling is false.
But do not fret,
you will land on love,
and although you'll stand a little lower,
you'll stand a little surer.

Dear one,
Worry not.
Your tears have been working for you
ever since they dropped.

-water for seed.

It is ok to spend the day crying;
it is the work that needs doing.
You've got to feel it before
you can free it.

Look at her.
Look at how she still pushes
hope in and out of her lungs.

-breathing is a badge of honour.

I lick my lips,
swallow and sigh.
I'm hoping you can translate it all.
I'm hoping you hear the prayers
of those who don't know what to say.

And then the silence kicked in,
and I wondered who would come for me.
Will anyone chase this loaded caravan headed deep?
But love did not let them see.
For love would not refuse the blooming of me.

Today is one of those days,
you know the kind when you must
muster up every ounce of courage your
frightened heart can find.

-letting go of us.

Once there was fire here;
a heat that warmed,
a spark of heart, a wink of light.
The flame died,
taking my fervour and my pride,
leaving ashy inquisitions inside.

I thought my questions were messy,
and my wonderings a sin.
Until love whispered tenderly,
'something's about to begin.'

-love is always up to something.

One cannot simply walk into the wilderness.
It is a place for the kidnapped;
those awakened by night,
and taken from their comfy beds.
Many will report them missing;
they are not where they used to be,
but it will soon be seen,
that the wild is where we are all meant to be.

Morning breaks to pour out the day,
and you, dear one, are made the same.
The world needs what your shattered heart,
can no longer safely contain.

Day asked night,
'What is a broken heart?'
Night answered day,
'When you discover your people,
 are not your people.'

-detours are for picking up new friends.

If weeping brought them nearer,
they'd be here by now.

Tell the clouds, my darling.
Send it up and let it turn to rain.

-what to do with the other side of the story.

Find a place to kneel,
and kneel there.

-what to do with the suffering.

Sometimes we ease into endings,
like the fade of twilight,
or the gradual turn of Summer to Fall.
Others come like lightning,
giving us no chance at farewell;
changing our lives mid-breath,
pulling from us any part that won't immediately let go.
Although one seems more merciful.
All are hard.
All linger, taking up space within.
One could say, it is human to know
goodbye is coming, but not be able to be ready for it.

THE COOLING OF COALS.

I thought possibility clothed herself in colour;
orchid purple, pear green, ocean blue.
Now I see, she wears sackcloth and sits in ashes.

-waking up.

The ground beneath the ground.

-where the waking happens.

Here begins the raking of ashes,
and I am forced to farewell
that which has long been a part of me.
All I can keep is what the truth fire
did not burn up.

I waited for others to empower me,
not knowing it is the work of ashes,
not knowing that the cooling of coals,
is the coming of courage.

-the making of me.

I understand,
you want to go back,
but even if you could
it would not be as good as it was,
or as fitting as it could have been before
everything changed.

-places become ghosts too.

It's warm in there.
I didn't notice I breathed stale air;
dying slowly of suffocation.
I didn't realise I gave you my power, my voice.
And still, you speak for me, but only in the room
where words circle because they cannot live in the sun.

Stop and say, 'This is where I am.
All these lessons are mine.
The seat in the shade is mine.
The view of the valley is mine.
The pang in my heart is mine.
They are all my teachers.'

There is always
a story before the story.

-learning not to mistake the seed for the tree.

Peace now,
It's only the exhale;
the learning.

We are like the ocean,
pushing on rocks,
wearing down impossibilities,
breaking as we do.

Though fog floats over sea,
waves keep rolling.
Though uncertainty makes it hard to see,
things come to us as they must.

You cannot speed up the moon,
or ease the hours before dawn;
the night is for holding on.
Wait, and let darkness work on you.

Surrender is the only way I know how to be strong.

It will not bloom in your hand.
You must put it down,
plant it deep,
leave it beneath the earth,
until beauty is willing to blossom for you.

The night is for settling,
all of our longings.
Here I lay my baby down.

-wild surrender.

Life is what you do with the 'could have been'.

Quiet now,
you don't have to fulfil expectations;
not even your own.

It's the smoke that gets me;
evidence of where I used to burn;
memories of when I lived in a dream.

-waiting for the heat to go out of it.

I asked for you,
but you would not come.
I don't know if it was your pride,
or angels intervening,
knowing what they know,
seeing as they do.

-praying for storms.

Alone on a sea of black,
without the company of stars,
I took what I could from time,
and let wounds turn into scars.

-sailing sorrow.

Why won't this wound stop weeping?
Maybe because it is deep and
there is much to learn, much to feel.
Maybe, from it flows rivers of light.

This is what you are made to do,
unfold in love,
continue to be renewed.
And when you move
not all will move too,
but it is well,
this is your breakthrough.

We know about the falling,
because we celebrate the rising,
but between them lives hours and hours
of wading through ashes.
Days of sitting with surrender.
Nobody likes to talk about that.

-silent Saturdays.

Pain is the hand that holds the lantern.

-what the shadows say.

And when the weather changes,
we run to open spaces,
to watch what rolls in.
For we know, storms always have something to say.

You can't outrun a storm.
You can't tame thunder.
Just be still,
be still in it.

-secret powers.

Release and receive,
Release and receive,
this is a beautiful rhythm;
this is a hard way of living.
To open your hand,
and take into your heart,
even in seasons of suffering.

Sometimes we must choose
between chains and change.
One binds,
the other births,
both are excruciating.

I gazed at stars
until the darkness
became beautiful,
and being on the outside
felt like home.

This place is sacred.
For under these stain glass skies,
I am surviving.
That is the miracle of me.

I spent time wondering how you sleep at night.
Then it came to me.
You've never been awake.
You're a sleepwalker, lost in your story.

-bliss.

Deal with it
before it deals you the life
you never wanted.

-forgive or die trying.

It could not have happened any other way.
We were who we were back then,
and knew no different.
I have made peace with the past now:
all the mistakes I made,
all your wrongs I forgave.
And if life swings wide, and we realign,
I know it will not be the same.
I have changed.
I have been schooled by heartbreak.
See my beautiful scars.

We are more than what we hold in our hands;
what we perceive with our senses.
The shaking told me so.

-lessons from the bathroom floor.

Answers do not heal,
unlike time and beauty,
and they are always with you.

When you feel it in your chest,
but don't see it with your eyes,
remember, the heart skips seasons,
and races time.

Do not grieve today,
what is for tomorrow.
We hear the storm before we drink the rain.

And I run deeper into the wilderness,
further from what is known,
to find who lives there,
and what lives in me.
And the only time I rest,
is to name the past or settle the future;
to bless what is and what will never be.

Years from now,
we will see,
what became of prayers,
what grew up under tears,
what surrender bravely brought forth.

I do not hope to rise.
I want to be buried alive,
taken under,
nourished in the deep.
The heights ping with glory noise,
the faff of earthly gain;
that is not where I find my food and drink.

-feasting on valley floors.

Night after night of sorrow.
Day after day of trying to make sense of it all.
This is the cooling;
the way wanting turns to thanking.

We are here to be wildlings;
to master thievery and ravage the wasteland.
Every thorn belongs to us.
They are our trials, our pains,
and we will use them to prick our skin,
creating holes where liberty can pour in.

Do you think all I see are cold coals?
The absence of embers?
The loss of light?
I cannot be fooled.
I dip my finger in,
and wipe it beneath my eyes;
warpaint, prepared for me.

-warrior

They say I must let go of the old,
before I can take hold of the new.
But what if it's a trick?
What if I am left empty-handed?
Still, I am suspicious of love;
I believe it has something up its sleeve.
This is how I surrender.
This is how I am strong.

There will always be disappointment.
Things hoped for but never held:
the cancellation of plans,
the breaking of promises,
the turning of hearts.
But through it all, and though we cry,
there is beauty,
there is music,
there is love.

Think love.
Think love.
Think love, my love.
This is your power;
the only way to be free.

-what the healers, the healed and the healing know.

Look at how she makes art of it all.
Every ending, a fallen flower,
bringing colour to earth.

The storm is a drumroll for the sunshine.

THE VALUE OF ASHES.

Scoop ashes into your hand.
Mix with tears.

-how to make beauty serum.

I am not impressed by your courage,
or your humility.
I merely marvel at what you must
have endured to show such beauty.

And one day soon,
But not too soon,
you will stop and say,
'This version of me
could not have arrived
any other way.'
And you will see all you lost
has been added to you.

Although I am a little blistered,
a little bruised,
the breaking put a part of me back together.

And if the day has brought you pain,
or been ruined by bad news,
finish it with kindness.
Hold your body.
Quiet your heart.
Turn your mind from hurtful thoughts.
For not a day is wasted when love is at work.

Beauty helped to make it better.

-in heart and mind.

Though few coins live in my pocket,
I can behold all the wonder I want.

-how to have a beautiful life.

Now and then, there will be a knock on your heart.
It is the past, delivering a package of pain.
Although one would think it wise not to open the door,
you must meet the uninvited on your doorstep.
You must thank him for his gift, and courageously
turn it into wild, beautiful things.

When prayers, so heavy, hit the floor.
Do not wade among them.
Leave them for the angels to pick at;
They will take what is needed to
paint a future for you.

I thought I came here to die;
this dip in the earth, an open grave;
until the rain arrived, and I saw
the pit was no less than a vessel,
given to catch a downpour.

These ashes tell the story of us;
they speak of the past and a possible future.

-rebuilding needs ruins.

I am grateful for locked doors.
They taught me to walk down hallways,
and out into the vast and beautiful.

-cheers to the outsiders.

Dear comfort,
I'm coming for you.
Kind regards,
Freedom.

Today I got a taste of you.
You weren't as satisfying as I remember.
Like two-day-old bread; dull,
unsuitable for a bright new morning.

See the wildflowers.
They will teach you how to succeed at being yourself.

-grow where you want to.

The state of my heart.
The span of my wings.
The depth of my unknowing.
The fragility of my certainties.
The strength of my spirit.

-things I did not know until I witnessed the wild place.

I hope you know the value of ashes,
and do not let them be stolen by the breeze.
But use them to build great cities of glory,
to write resurrection stories,
and make monuments to what you believe.

Goodbye.
The most confusing word.
To wish well before tearing hearts.
To declare departing virtuous,
though tears spill and hearts ache.
Maybe we should say instead.
I see the sun in the moon, or
I taste the honey in the poison, or
I feel the love in pain.

Though there is doubt,
and doubting tears,
the sting of lost hope and wasted years,
there standing upright in the desert wind,
is an army of miracles,
a forest of kin.

Love is in yesterday;
in the hour I saw you last.
Love is present here,
though I don't always sense
the many ways you come to me.
Love is in tomorrow,
preparing rooms and hearts to walk into.
Love is in it all:
the blur of memories,
the breath of certainties,
the blink of possibilities.

The sun rises with no promise of staying,
And I am glad,
for holding such a vow
would deny me the stars.

-words I could not say at first.

You cannot simply wish and pray the cage away.
You must fly out.
You must trade familiar songs for lonely branches.
You have to get a little lost to find your heart.
At first, it will feel like you're losing.
The wind will smack your face
before it assists your wings.
But brave on.
You will find a current of flow,
and finally know the freedom of being yourself.

When pain becomes wings.

-my favourite season.

Each mourning says the same thing,
'Look ahead.'

-the hardest thing on my 'to do' list.

Mostly I am too busy for mystery.
But when I stop,
oh, when I stop,
the silence sings a mighty chorus,
and I sense that something
magnificent is going on.

We can do no better than ink on paper,
then piling up glass and stone and wood,
building that which has no heart, no lungs.
But Love, Love writes with living things.
It bursts through time and space,
showing us that what we call coincidence,
is nothing less than the creeping of destiny.

Why wrestle for room in the nest
when all the wild is yours?

Leaving feels like taking in ocean air
after years of breathing under blankets.

-I didn't know what I was missing.

Rain on tin applauds me;
I made it through the dry season.
It took years of sky watching,
of saying, 'It's about to storm.'
Until, one day,
it started to patter,
and I knew,
there is no holding back
what is meant for me.

Be not darkened by silence,
nor silenced by darkness.
The day will come,
and bring with it,
heat and colour and beauty.

Life gives us signs and time,
dots and lines.
Although it seems messy,
the years are connected;
they are pathways to strength,
set to bring us full circle.

These four words
we long to say and mean.
'It was worth it.'
All the toiling and tears.
All the days, months and years
gave us gold;
if not in our pockets,
then in our hearts.

Draw a heart around it,
and colour it in.

-how I fix mistakes on the page and in the past.

I cannot hold what wants to run.
What is mine is free to come.

Now that my parachute has opened,
I can see it is good that I am falling.
For I am in the hands of the wind;
Spirit fills my sail.

And oh that day,
that blessed day,
when I saw my blindness.
When I saw how I plucked my feathers
to pad a nest when I could have used them to fly.

I once sang of love
and talked of freedom.
Until I discovered,
they are best lived.

I learnt to look for little pops of joy,
instead of waiting to be happy.

-how to change your life.

Watered by words.
Warmed by wonder,
the heart finds a way
to dissolve the pain.

I am thankful for the arrows,
they helped me find my heart.

This is the road;
the way open for me.
It is not the slightest,
nor the most scenic route,
but it is mine,
and I will take from this trail all I can,
for tomorrow the view will change,
and I will need what can only be foraged here.

How lovely is the sunrise song,
the turn from night to day.
To see the light gently infuse;
to watch the darkness fade.
How lovely is the sunrise song,
when hope is not deferred.
To feel the morning place in your hands,
what you have long heard.

Awakened,
I see burning bushes everywhere;
in both the presence and absence of things hoped for.
And I, content to leave lost dreams,
warm my heart over a new flame,
and revel in the thought of living
many lives in one lifetime.

Glory needs ashes.

The first time I lost my leaves
I thought I was dying.
I waited all winter,
enduring the numb of midnight, and frost at dawn,
until the sun started to set differently,
and the breeze began to feel a little more hopeful.
I wish someone told me
life is a twisted coil of beginnings and ends;
that living is changing,
and dying is a way we each get to bless the earth.

I see how she holds on.
Waiting for winter to fold,
waiting for warmth; permission to bloom.
She knows it's coming.
She knows soon sunshine will open her up,
and from her core will flow streams
of living colour.

Oh, lovely light, where have you been?
Hiding so you can surprise me?
Withholding so you can delight me?
Leaving the darkness so I could see,
courage abundant that lives in me?
Did you depart so the night could purge,
all that prevents sweet freedom's birth?
Oh, lovely light, where have you been?

If you climb to the top of a mountain,
love is there to meet you.
If you sink to the bottom of the ocean,
love got there before you.
Love is in the water and in the air.
It hikes further, fly's higher, falls deeper than you can.
So wander where you want, with no fear of losing
love.

And then I saw love relax.
Like it knew something I couldn't grasp.
And I figured it must be bigger, deeper, wiser
than I had given credit.

Forgiveness is the fairest of them all.

ABOUT THE AUTHOR

Lauren Lott lives in Lake Macquarie, NSW, Australia. In October 2020 her first collection of poetry and prose, 'The Remains of Burning.' was published.

Lauren is currently working on a second collection, to be released in 2021.

To contact or stay connected, follow Lauren on Instagram @llott.writes